igloobooks

Published in 2016
by Igloo Books Ltd
Cottage Farm
Sywell
NN6 0BJ
www.igloobooks.com

Food photography and recipe development
© Stockfood, The Food Media Agency

Cover image: © imageBROKER / Alamy Stock Photo

Cover designed by Nicholas Gage
Edited by Natalie Baker

LEO002 0916
2 4 6 8 10 9 7 5 3 1
ISBN 978-1-78670-151-0

Printed and manufactured in China

CONTENTS

Disclaimer: for recipes that require a slow cooker, the reader can substitute this for a lidded ovenproof dish and cook for the same cooking time in the oven.

EASY

MINESTRONE SOUP

SERVES
4

PREPARATION TIME: 15 MINUTES
COOKING TIME: 40 MINUTES

4 tbsp olive oil

2 cloves garlic, minced

2 large carrots, peeled and sliced

2 large sticks celery, sliced

1 tbsp tomato purée

400g / 14 oz / 2 cups butter beans

400g / 14 oz / 2 cups garden peas, frozen

500 ml / 1 pint / 2 ¼ cups vegetable stock

1 bay leaf

2 tbsp basil leaves, finely chopped

GARNISH

4 sprigs of basil leaves

METHOD

- Heat the olive oil in a large casserole dish over a medium heat until hot.

- Sweat the garlic, carrot, celery and bay leaf with a little salt for 8–10 minutes until they start to soften, stirring occasionally.

- Stir through the tomato purée, then spoon everything into a large saucepan.

- Add the butter beans and peas and cover with the stock.

- Cook on a low setting for 30 minutes until tender.

- Discard the bay leaf and adjust the seasoning to taste.

- Stir through the chopped basil then spoon into serving bowls

- Garnish with sprigs of basil leaves before serving.

CAULIFLOWER SOUP

SERVES
4

PREPARATION TIME: 5 MINUTES
COOKING TIME: 30 MINUTES

2 tbsp olive oil

2 tbsp butter

3 leeks, finely chopped

2 cloves of garlic, crushed

1 cauliflower, cubed

1 litre / 1 pint 15 fl. oz / 4 cups vegetable stock

100 ml / 3 ½ fl. oz / ½ cup double (heavy) cream

¼ tsp freshly ground nutmeg

flat leaf parsley to garnish

METHOD

- Heat the oil and butter in a saucepan and fry the leeks for 8 minutes or until softened.

- Add the garlic and cauliflower to the pan and cook for 2 more minutes, then stir in the vegetable stock and bring to the boil.

- Simmer for 15 minutes then stir in the double cream and nutmeg.

- Blend the soup until smooth with a liquidiser or immersion blender then try the soup and adjust the seasoning with salt and pepper.

LEEK SOUP

SERVES
4

PREPARATION TIME: 5 MINUTES
COOKING TIME: 20 MINUTES

2 tbsp butter

4 leeks, thickly sliced

1 litre / 1 pint 15 fl. oz / 4 cups good quality vegetable stock

100 ml / 3 ½ fl. oz / ½ cup double (heavy) cream

¼ tsp nutmeg, freshly grated

parsley to garnish

METHOD

• Heat the butter in a sauté pan and fry the leeks for 5 minutes, stirring occasionally.

• Stir in the vegetable stock and simmer for 15 minutes or until the leeks are tender.

• Stir in the cream and nutmeg, then taste the soup and adjust the seasoning with salt and pepper.

• Ladle into four warm bowls and serve garnished with parsley.

POTATO AND BACON SOUP

SERVES
4

PREPARATION TIME: 15 MINUTES
COOKING TIME: 4 HOURS

2 large white potatoes, peeled and finely diced

500 ml / 18 fl. oz / 2 cups vegetable stock

1 bay leaf

1 sprig thyme

GARNISH

crispy bacon, pre-cooked

fresh chives, chopped

METHOD

- Heat the olive oil in a large saucepan set over a medium heat.

- Add the potato and sweat for 10 minutes until the potato starts to soften.

- Add the bay leaf, thyme and stock and stir well.

- Pour into a slow cooker and cook on a low setting for 4 hours.

- Adjust the seasoning after 4 hours and ladle into warm soup bowls.

- Garnish with the pre-cooked crispy bacon and chives.

- Serve immediately.

CREAM OF ORANGE LENTIL SOUP

SERVES
4

PREPARATION TIME: 10 MINUTES
COOKING TIME: 4 HOURS 20 MINUTES

2 tbsp olive oil

225 g / 8 oz / 1 ¼ cups orange split lentils

1 onion, finely chopped

1 clove garlic, minced

1 tsp cumin seeds, toasted

1 tsp ground cumin

½ tsp ground coriander seeds

500 ml / 18 fl. oz / 2 cups vegetable stock

125 ml / 4 ½ fl. oz / ½ cup carrot juice

125ml / 4 ½ fl. oz / ½ cup double
(heavy) cream

GARNISH

coriander (cilantro) leaves

METHOD

- Heat the olive oil in a large saucepan and sweat the onion and garlic with a little salt for 5 minutes.

- Add the ground cumin, ground coriander and cumin seeds, stirring well.

- Add the lentils and cover with the stock.

- Pour everything into a slow cooker and cook on a low setting for 4 hours until the lentils have absorbed most of the stock and are soft and tender.

- Once ready, stir through the carrot juice and cream and adjust the seasoning to taste.

- Pour the soup into a large saucepan and blitz until smooth using a stick blender.

- Reheat the soup over a medium heat until hot, stirring frequently.

- Spoon the soup into serving bowls and garnish each with a sprig of coriander.

CHUNKY BACON AND VEGETABLE SOUP

SERVES
4

PREPARATION TIME: 5 MINUTES
COOKING TIME: 30 MINUTES

2 tbsp olive oil

2 tbsp butter

1 onion, finely chopped

2 cloves of garlic, crushed

2 medium potatoes, cubed

3 carrots, cubed

1 litre / 1 pint 15 fl. oz / 4 cups vegetable stock

150 g / 5 ½ oz / 1 cup peas, defrosted if frozen

4 rashers streaky bacon

a few sprigs of chervil to serve

METHOD

• Heat the oil and butter in a saucepan and fry the onion for 5 minutes or until softened.

• Add the garlic, potatoes and carrots to the pan and cook for 2 more minutes, then stir in the vegetable stock and bring to the boil.

• Simmer for 12 minutes then add the peas and simmer for a further 5 minutes.

• While the peas are cooking, cook the bacon under a hot grill until crispy then chop into large pieces.

• Stir the bacon into the soup, add salt and pepper to taste and garnish with chervil.

CREAM OF COURGETTE SOUP

SERVES
4

PREPARATION TIME: 15 MINUTES
COOKING TIME: 3 HOURS 20–25 MINUTES

30 ml / 1 fl. oz / 2 tbsp sesame oil

2 large courgettes, diced

1 leek, finely sliced and washed

500 ml / 18 fl. oz / 2 cups vegetable stock

4 rice noodle nests

125 ml / 4 ½ fl. oz / ½ cup double (heavy) cream

salt and pepper

GARNISH

2 tbsp sesame seeds

12 water biscuits/crackers

METHOD

• Heat the sesame oil in a large saucepan set over a medium heat.

• Sweat the leek and courgette for 8–10 minutes, stirring occasionally, until softened.

• Add the stock then pour everything into a slow cooker.

• Cook on a low setting for 3 hours.

• Pour back into a saucepan and add the cream, stirring well.

• Cook over a medium heat for a few minutes before puréeing with a stick blender until smooth.

• Adjust the seasoning to taste and keep warm over a low heat.

• Blanch the rice noodles in a large saucepan of boiling, salted water for 1 minute until soft.

• Drain and reserve to one side.

• Ladle the soup into warm bowls and sit a rice noodle nest in the middle of the soup.

• Garnish with a sprinkle of sesame seeds before serving.

ORANGE LENTIL AND HAZELNUT SOUP

SERVES
4

PREPARATION TIME: 10 MINUTES

COOKING TIME: 4 HOURS

2 tbsp olive oil

225 g / 8 oz / 1 ¼ cups orange split lentils

1 onion, finely chopped

1 clove garlic, minced

750 ml / 1 pint 6 fl. oz / 3 cups vegetable stock

1 bay leaf

GARNISH

110 g / 4 oz / ¼ cup hazelnuts

METHOD

- Heat the olive oil in a large saucepan set over a medium heat.

- Sweat the onion, garlic and bay leaf with a little salt for 5-6 minutes, stirring occasionally, until translucent and softened.

- Add the lentils and cover with the stock.

- Pour everything into a slow cooker and cook on a low setting for 4 hours until the lentils have absorbed ⬜ of the stock and are soft and tender.

- Adjust the seasoning to taste and keep warm to one side.

- Lightly toast the hazelnuts in a dry frying pan set over a medium heat until they start to release their aroma.

- Roughly chop the hazelnuts and season to taste.

- Spoon the soup into serving bowls and garnish with the toasted hazelnuts on top before serving.

MUSHROOM THYME SOUP

SERVES
4

PREPARATION TIME: 10 MINUTES
COOKING TIME: 25 MINUTES

2 tbsp olive oil, plus extra to garnish

2 tbsp butter

1 onion, finely chopped

2 cloves of garlic, crushed

2 tbsp fresh thyme leaves

400 g / 14 oz / 5 ⅓ cups mushrooms, chopped

1 litre / 1 pint 15 fl. oz / 4 cups vegetable stock

100 ml / 3 ½ fl. oz / ½ cup double (heavy) cream

4 fresh thyme sprigs, to garnish

salt and freshly ground black pepper

METHOD

• Heat the oil and butter in a saucepan and fry the onion for 5 minutes or until softened.

• Add the garlic and mushrooms to the pan and cook for 5 more minutes.

• Stir in the vegetable stock and bring to the boil. Simmer for 15 minutes then stir in the double cream and nutmeg.

• Blend the soup until smooth with a liquidiser or immersion blender, then taste for seasoning and adjust with salt and pepper.

• Ladle into warm bowls and top each one with a drizzle of olive oil and a sprig of fresh thyme.

CARROT SOUP

SERVES
4

PREPARATION TIME: 5 MINUTES
COOKING TIME: 30 MINUTES

2 tbsp olive oil

2 tbsp butter

1 onion, finely chopped

2 garlic cloves, crushed

4 carrots, julienned

½ tsp ground cumin, plus extra to sprinkle

1 litre / 1 pint 15 fl. oz / 4 cups vegetable stock

2 tbsp mint leaves, finely chopped

METHOD

• Heat the oil and butter in a saucepan and fry the onion for 8 minutes or until softened.

• Add the garlic, carrots and cumin to the pan and cook for 2 more minutes, then stir in the vegetable stock and bring to the boil.

• Simmer for 20 minutes or until the carrots are tender. Remove a large spoonful of carrots from the pan with a slotted spoon and reserve for garnish, then blend the rest until smooth with a liquidiser or immersion blender.

• Taste the soup and adjust the seasoning with salt and pepper, then stir in half of the mint and divide between 4 warm bowls.

• Top with the reserved carrots, the rest of the mint and a final sprinkle of cumin.

EASY

TOMATO THYME SOUP

SERVES
4

PREPARATION TIME: 5 MINUTES
COOKING TIME: 30 MINUTES

2 tbsp olive oil

1 onion, finely chopped

4 cloves of garlic, crushed

2 tbsp thyme leaves

450 g / 1 lb ripe tomatoes, diced

500 ml / 17 ½ fl. oz / 2 cups vegetable stock

METHOD

• Heat the oil in a saucepan and fry the onion for 8 minutes or until softened.

• Add the garlic and half of the thyme to the pan and cook for 2 more minutes, then stir in the tomatoes and vegetable stock and bring to the boil.

• Simmer for 20 minutes then blend until smooth with a liquidiser or immersion blender.

• Taste the soup and adjust the seasoning with salt and pepper, then ladle into bowls and sprinkle with the rest of the thyme.

CREAMY PEA SOUP

SERVES
4

PREPARATION TIME: 5 MINUTES
COOKING TIME: 15 MINUTES

2 tbsp olive oil

2 tbsp butter

1 onion, finely chopped

2 garlic cloves, crushed

400 g / 14 oz peas, defrosted if frozen

1 litre / 1 pint 15 fl. oz / 4 cups vegetable stock

100 ml / 3 ½ fl. oz / ½ cup double (heavy) cream

1 tbsp mint leaves, finely chopped

METHOD

• Heat the oil and butter in a saucepan and fry the onion for 5 minutes or until softened.

• Add the garlic and peas to the pan and cook for 2 more minutes, then stir in the vegetable stock and bring to the boil.

• Simmer for 5 minutes then stir in the double cream and mint.

• Blend the soup until smooth with a liquidiser or immersion blender then try the soup and adjust the seasoning with salt and pepper.

• Ladle into warm bowls and sprinkle with black pepper.

NOODLE SOUP

SERVES
4

PREPARATION TIME: 10 MINUTES
COOKING TIME: 15–20 MINUTES

1 tbsp olive oil

1 onion, peeled and finely chopped

1 celery stalk, finely chopped

1 carrot, peeled and finely chopped

1 clove of garlic, finely chopped

1 L / 2 pints / 5 cups chicken stock

80g / 3 oz / ¼ cup spaghetti

1 nutmeg

salt and pepper

2 tbsp Parmesan cheese, grated

extra virgin olive oil

METHOD

• Heat the olive oil in a pan.

• Add the onion, celery and carrot and sweat until softened.

• Add the garlic and cook for a further minute.

• Pour in the stock and bring to a simmer.

• Break the pasta into lots of small pieces.

• Add the pasta and cook until 'al dente' or just tender.

• Grate over a little nutmeg and adjust the seasoning.

• Serve with Parmesan cheese and oil for drizzling.

MANGO SWEET SOUP

SERVES
4

PREPARATION TIME: 15 MINUTES
COOKING TIME: 4 HOURS 15–20 MINUTES

110 g / 4 oz / 1 cup tapioca, soaked in cold
water overnight then drained

1 ¼ l / 2 pints 4 fl. oz / 5 cups whole milk

110 g / 4 oz / 1 cup caster (superfine) sugar

55 g / 2 oz / ½ stick unsalted butter, cubed

a pinch of salt

1 large mango, de-stoned and flesh finely diced

2 eating pears, peeled, cored and finely diced

1 mandarin, peeled, skinned and finely diced

TO GARNISH

2 mandarins, zest pared and julienned

METHOD

- Combine the tapioca, milk, sugar and salt in a large saucepan.

- Cook over a low heat, stirring frequently until the tapioca starts to absorb the milk and swell in size.

- Add the butter gradually to the pudding and continue cooking over a low heat, stirring constantly until the butter has been absorbed into the pudding.

- Fold through the pear and pour into a slow cooker.

- Cover with a lid and cook on a medium setting for 4 hours until the tapioca is thickened and creamy.

- Add the mango and mandarin flesh and stir thoroughly before spooning into serving bowls.

- Garnish with the julienned mandarin peel before serving.

MEAT

MEXICAN SOUP

SERVES
4

PREPARATION TIME: 15 MINUTES
COOKING TIME: 3 HOURS

3 tbsp sunflower oil

2 chicken breasts cut into large chunks

2 onion, chopped

2 cloves garlic, minced

675 g / 1 lb 8 oz / 5 cups sweetcorn, drained

1.2 l / 2 pints / 4 ⁴/₅ cups chicken stock, hot

2 ½ tsp dried oregano

2 tsp chilli (chili) powder

2 tsp paprika

GARNISH

1 tbsp coriander (cilantro) leaves

METHOD

• Heat most of the oil in a large frying pan set over a moderate heat until hot.

• Season the chicken and seal in batches until deep golden. Remove from the pan and reduce the heat.

• Add the remaining oil to the pan and sweat the onion and garlic for 5–6 minutes with a little salt, stirring occasionally. Add the ground spices and stir well.

• Spoon into a slow cooker, then add the chicken, sweetcorn and stock.

• Cook on a low setting for 3 hours until the chicken is cooked and tender.

• Adjust the seasoning to taste before spooning everything into a serving pot.

• Garnish with the coriander and chilli before serving.

MULLIGATAWNY SOUP

SERVES
4

PREPARATION TIME: 15 MINUTES
COOKING TIME: 4 HOURS

2 tbsp butter, unsalted

2 tbsp olive oil

1 leek, trimmed, sliced and washed

500 ml / 18 fl. oz / 2 cups coconut milk

500 ml / 18 fl. oz / 2 cups chicken stock

2 chicken breasts, diced

2 sticks celery, peeled and sliced

2 tsp ground cumin

2 tsp ground coriander seeds

½ tsp garam masala

30 g / 1 oz / ¼ cup flaked (slivered) almonds, toasted

METHOD

• Melt the butter with the olive oil in a large, heavy-based saucepan set over a moderate heat.

• Sweat the leek and celery for 5-6 minutes, stirring occasionally, until they start to soften.

• Add the spices at this point along with 1 tsp of salt and stir well.

• Stir in the coconut milk and chicken stock, then pour into a slow cooker.

• Cook on a low setting for 4 hours.

• Adjust the seasoning to taste after 4 hours.

• Spoon into balti dishes and garnish with the almonds and some black pepper.

• Serve immediately.

PARMESAN SOUP

SERVES
4

PREPARATION TIME: 5 MINUTES
COOKING TIME: 15 MINUTES

1.5 l / 2 pints 12 fl. oz / 6 cups chicken stock

2 eggs

2 tbsp Parmesan cheese, grated

bunch basil leaves

250 g / 9 oz / 2 cups spinach leaves, shredded

salt and pepper

nutmeg

METHOD

- Bring the chicken stock to the boil in a pan.

- Whisk together the eggs, Parmesan and basil until completely blended.

- Lower the heat. Whisking constantly in a figure of eight motion, stir the egg mixture into the stock a little at a time until all is incorporated.

- Leave to simmer very gently for about 5 minutes until thickened.

- Stir through the spinach and a little grated nutmeg.

- Adjust the seasoning before serving.

THAI RED CURRY SOUP

SERVES
4

PREPARATION TIME: 15 MINUTES
COOKING TIME: 4 HOURS

2 tbsp groundnut oil

4 chicken breasts, sliced

4 shallots, finely sliced

2 cloves of garlic, minced

5 cm (2 in) ginger, peeled and minced

2 red chillies, deseeded and finely sliced

500 ml / 18 fl. oz / 2 cups chicken stock

4 rice noodle nests

1 lime, juiced

1 tbsp fish sauce

1 tbsp dark soy sauce

METHOD

- Combine half of the oil with the red chilli, garlic, ginger, soy sauce and lime juice in a food processor. Pulse until smooth.

- Heat the remaining oil in a large casserole dish set over a medium heat.

- Sweat the shallots with the paste for 4–5 minutes, stirring frequently.

- Add the chicken stock and the chicken and stir well.

- Pour into a slow cooker and add the rice noodle nests, making sure they are soaked in the liquid. Cook on a low setting for 4 hours.

- Adjust the seasoning after 4 hours using fish sauce, salt and pepper.

- Ladle into warm soup bowls and serve immediately.

LENTIL SOUP WITH TOMATOES

SERVES
6

PREPARATION TIME: 10 MINUTES
COOKING TIME: 4 HOURS

2 tbsp vegetable oil

1 onion, finely chopped

2 cloves garlic, minced

225 g / 8 oz / 1 ¼ cups
orange split lentils

500 ml / 18 fl oz / 2 cups
vegetable stock

175 g / 6 oz / 1 cup cherry
tomatoes, halved

GARNISH

110 g / 4 oz / ¼ cup chorizo, sliced

2 tbsp coriander (cilantro) leaves, chopped

METHOD

- Heat the oil in a large saucepan set over a moderate heat.

- Sweat the onion and garlic for 5–6 minutes, stirring occasionally, until they start to soften.

- Add the lentils and stir well.

- Cover with the stock, then pour everything into a slow cooker.

- Cook on a low setting for 4 hours until the lentils have absorbed the stock.

- Add the tomatoes after 4 hours and continue to cook for 30 minutes.

- Adjust the seasoning to taste and keep on a low setting as you prepare the garnish.

- Preheat the grill to hot and grill the chorizo slices for a minute on both sides until crisp.

- Drain on kitchen paper.

- Ladle the soup into warm bowls and garnish with the coriander and chorizo slices before serving.

PARSNIP SOUP WITH PANCETTA

SERVES
4

PREPARATION TIME: 15 MINUTES
COOKING TIME: 3 HOURS 30 MINUTES

2 tbsp butter

2 tbsp olive oil

1 kg / 2 lbs 4 oz / 6 ½ cups, peeled and diced

1 clove garlic, minced

500 ml / 18 fl. oz / 2 cups vegetable stock

250 ml / 9 fl. oz / 1 cup milk

4 tbsp double (heavy) cream

GARNISH

8 rashers pancetta

pinch ground white pepper

METHOD

- Melt the butter with the olive oil in a large saucepan.

- Add the garlic and parsnip and sweat with a little salt for 15–20 minutes, stirring occasionally.

- Spoon everything into a slow cooker and cover with the stock and milk. Cook on a low setting for 3 hours.

- After 3 hours, pour everything back into a saucepan and purée using a stick blender until smooth.

- Add the double cream and simmer the soup as you prepare the garnish. Preheat the grill to high.

- Line a tray with greaseproof paper and line with the pancetta. Grill for 3–4 minutes until golden and crisp.

- Remove from the grill and drain on kitchen paper.

- Adjust the seasoning of the soup if necessary then ladle into serving bowls.

- Garnish with rashers of pancetta and a pinch of ground white pepper before serving.

ITALIAN RUSTIC TOMATO SOUP

SERVES
4

PREPARATION TIME: 15 MINUTES
COOKING TIME: 30–35 MINUTES

2 tbsp olive oil

1 onion, peeled and chopped

1 carrot, peeled and finely chopped

1 celery stalk, finely chopped

2 cloves of garlic, chopped

1 courgette (zucchini), finely chopped

2 potatoes, peeled and finely chopped

2 slices Parma ham, chopped

400 g / 14 oz / 2 cups canned chopped tomatoes

1 dried red chilli (chili), chopped

1 l / 1 pint 16 fl. oz / 4 cups chicken stock

salt and pepper

extra virgin olive oil

METHOD

- Heat the oil in a pan and sweat the onion, carrot and celery without colouring.

- Add the garlic and cook for 2 minutes until soft.

- Add the courgettes and potatoes, stir well and leave to soften for a 5–10 minutes, then add the ham.

- Pour in the tomatoes, crumble in a little of the chilli, then stir in the stock.

- Bring to a simmer and leave to cook until the vegetables are tender – about 20 minutes.

- Taste and adjust the seasoning if necessary, adding chilli if desired.

- Roughly mash the vegetables with a potato masher or pulse in a liquidiser

- Serve drizzled with olive oil.

SWEETCORN AND BACON CHOWDER

SERVES
4

PREPARATION TIME: 10 MINUTES
COOKING TIME: 20 MINUTES

2 tbsp butter

1 onion, finely chopped

6 thick slices smoked streaky bacon

3 sweetcorn cobs

1 large potato, peeled and diced

500 ml / 17 ½ fl. oz / 2 cups ham
or chicken stock

500 ml / 17 ½ fl. oz / 2 cups milk

30 g / 1 oz / ½ cup popcorn

METHOD

- Heat the butter in a saucepan and fry the onion and bacon for 5 minutes.

- Hold the corn cobs vertically on a chopping board and cut down with a sharp knife to release the sweetcorn kernels.

- Add them to the pan with the potato, stock and milk and simmer for 15 minutes.

- Ladle half of the soup into a liquidiser and blend until smooth, then stir it back into the pan.

- Ladle the chowder into warm bowls and top with the popcorn just before serving.

CHORIZO SOUP

SERVES
4

PREPARATION TIME: 15 MINUTES
COOKING TIME: 4 HOURS

2 tbsp olive oil

1 onion, finely chopped

2 cloves garlic, minced

2 rashers smokey bacon, chopped

225 g / 8 oz / ½ cup canned
kidney beans, drained

450 g / 1 lb / 1 cup canned
haricot beans, drained

110 g / 4 oz / ¼ cup chorizo, cut into thin strips

4 tomatoes, chopped

500 ml / 18 fl. oz / 2 cups vegetable stock

METHOD

- Heat the olive oil in a large casserole dish set over a medium heat until hot.

- Sauté the onion, garlic and bacon with a little salt for 6-7 minutes, stirring occasionally until the onion has softened.

- Add the canned beans, chorizo, stock, tomatoes and seasoning and stir well.

- Pour into a slow cooker and cook on a low setting for 4 hours until the beans are tender and have absorbed the stock to leave you with a thickened soup.

- Adjust the seasoning to taste before ladling into warm soup bowls.

- Serve immediately.

MACARONI SOUP

SERVES
4

PREPARATION TIME: 20 MINUTES
COOKING TIME: 1½ HOURS

2 tbsp olive oil

50 g / 1 ½ oz / ⅕ cup pancetta

1 onion, peeled and finely chopped

2 celery stalks, finely chopped

2 carrots, peeled and finely chopped

2 cloves of garlic, finely chopped

2 potatoes, peeled and finely chopped

2 tomatoes, peeled and finely chopped

1.5 L / 2 ½ pints / 5 ½ cups chicken stock

100 g / 3 ½ oz / ½ cup macaroni pasta

salt and pepper

Parmesan cheese

METHOD

- Heat the oil in a large pan and fry off the pancetta until the fat runs and it starts to turn golden.

- Add the vegetables in the order above, giving each one a good 5 minutes to cook without colouring, stirring regularly, before adding the next one.

- Pour in the stock and bring to a gentle simmer, then cook very gently for about an hour.

- Add the pasta and cook for a further 30 minutes.

- Adjust the seasoning.

- Serve warm, sprinkled with Parmesan and drizzled with olive oil.

YELLOW PEPPER SOUP

SERVES
4

PREPARATION TIME: 5 MINUTES
COOKING TIME: 40 MINUTES

1 ciabatta loaf

olive oil

25 g / 1 oz butter

1 onion, finely chopped

1 clove of garlic, finely chopped

4 yellow peppers, finely chopped

750 ml / 1 ¼ pints / 3 cups chicken stock

120 ml / 4 fl oz / ½ cup double (heavy) cream

salt and pepper

METHOD

• Preheat the oven to 180°C / 350F / gas 5. Tear the ciabatta into large croutons and toss with olive oil. Place on a baking sheet.

• Bake in the oven for 10–12 minutes, until golden and crunchy and then set aside on kitchen paper.

• Heat the butter in a pan, then sweat the onion and garlic without colouring.

• Add the peppers and cook for a further 10 minutes until they have softened.

• Pour over the stock and simmer for 25 minutes, until the peppers are completely tender.

• Allow to cool slightly and then whiz in a liquidiser until smooth.

• Transfer back to the pan and stir in the cream, heating gently.

• Adjust the seasoning before serving.

LENTIL AND SAUSAGE SOUP

SERVES
4

PREPARATION TIME: 15 MINUTES
COOKING TIME: 6 HOURS 10 MINUTES

30 ml / 1 fl. oz / 2 tbsp olive oil

1 bulb of garlic, lightly crushed

2 carrots, peeled and sliced

1 leek, halved and washed

400 g / 14 oz / 2 cups puy lentils

300 g / 10 ½ oz / 2 cups Charlotte potatoes, peeled and turned

250 g / 9 oz / 1 ¾ cups smoked sausage, chopped

1.2 l / 2 pints / 4 ⅘ cups vegetables stock

2 bay leaves

salt and pepper

METHOD

• Heat the olive oil in a large casserole dish set over a medium heat until hot.

• Sauté the leek, garlic, carrots and bay leaves with a little salt for a few minutes.

• Add the sausage, lentils and potatoes and stir well.

• Cover with the stock before pouring into a slow cooker.

• Cover with a lid and cook on a medium setting for 6 hours.

• Adjust the seasoning to taste after 6 hours before ladling into serving bowls and serving.

MOROCCAN SOUP

SERVES
4

PREPARATION TIME: 20 MINUTES
COOKING TIME: 6 HOURS

4 tbsp olive oil

450 g / 1 lb / 3 cups lamb, diced

400 g / 14 oz / 2 cups canned chickpeas
(garbanzo beans), drained

400 g / 14 oz / 2 cups chopped tomatoes

110g / 4 oz / 1 cup peas

1 onion, chopped

2 carrots, peeled and sliced

3 sticks celery, sliced

2 cloves garlic, minced

1 tbsp harissa

500ml / 18 fl. oz / 2 cups lamb stock

METHOD

- Coat the lamb in half of the olive oil and season generously.

- Heat a large casserole dish over a moderate heat until hot.

- Seal the lamb in batches until golden brown.

- Transfer to a slow cooker and reduce the heat under the dish a little.

- Add the remaining olive oil and sauté the onion, garlic and carrots for a few minutes.

- Stir well then add the harissa and chickpeas.

- Stir thoroughly before adding the stock, chopped tomatoes, peas and seasoning.

- Pour into the slow cooker and cover with a lid.

- Cook on a medium setting for 6 hours. Adjust the seasoning before ladling into serving bowls.

- Garnish with coriander before serving.

VEGETARIAN

PENNE MINESTRONE SOUP

SERVES
4

PREPARATION TIME: 15 MINUTES

COOKING TIME: 3 HOURS

4 tbsp olive oil

2 cloves garlic, minced

2 white potatoes, peeled and finely diced

2 large sticks celery, sliced

2 large carrots, peeled and sliced

110g / 4 oz / 1 ¼ cups penne

1 tbsp tomato purée

568 ml / 1 pint / 2 ¼ cups vegetable stock

1 bay leaf

GARNISH

4 sprigs of basil leaves

METHOD

- Heat the olive oil in a large casserole dish over a medium heat until hot.

- Sweat the potatoes, garlic, carrot, celery and bay leaf with a little salt for 8–10 minutes until they start to soften, stirring occasionally.

- Stir through the tomato purée, then spoon everything into a slow cooker.

- Add the pasta and cover with the stock.

- Cook on a low setting for 3 hours until the pasta is tender.

- Discard the bay leaf and adjust the seasoning to taste.

- Spoon into serving bowls and garnish with sprigs of basil leaves before serving.

LEEK AND POTATO SOUP

SERVES
4

PREPARATION TIME: 15 MINUTES
COOKING TIME: 4 HOURS

2 tbsp olive oil

1 leek, sliced

2 large white potatoes, peeled and finely diced

500 ml / 18 fl. oz / 2 cups vegetable stock

1 bay leaf

1 sprig thyme

GARNISH

30 g / 1 oz / ¼ Parmesan, shaved

METHOD

- Heat the olive oil in a large saucepan set over a medium heat.

- Sweat the leek for 4–5 minutes with a little salt, stirring frequently, then add the potato and continue to sweat for 10 minutes until the potato starts to soften.

- Add the bay leaf, thyme and stock and stir well.

- Pour into a slow cooker and cook on a low setting for 4 hours.

- Adjust the seasoning after 4 hours and ladle into warm soup bowls.

- Garnish with the shaved Parmesan.

- Serve immediately.

RATATOUILLE SOUP

SERVES
4

PREPARATION TIME: 5 MINUTES
COOKING TIME: 35 MINUTES

2 tbsp olive oil

1 onion, finely chopped

1 large carrot, diced

1 courgette (zucchini), diced

½ small butternut squash, peeled,
seeded and diced

1 tbsp herbes de Provence

2 cloves of garlic, finely chopped

600 ml / 1 pint / 2 ½ cups vegetable stock

400 g / 14 oz / 2 cups canned
tomatoes, chopped

4 small balls mozzarella

4 basil leaves

salt and pepper

METHOD

• Heat the oil in a large saucepan and fry the onion, carrot, courgette and squash for 10 minutes without browning. Add the herbes de Provence and garlic and fry for 2 more minutes.

• Pour in the stock and tomatoes then simmer for 20 minutes or until the carrots and squash are tender. Taste the soup and adjust the seasoning with salt and black pepper.

• Ladle into four warm bowls and top each one with a mozzarella ball and a basil leaf before serving.

CHANNA DAL SOUP

SERVES
4

PREPARATION TIME: 15 MINUTES
COOKING TIME: 4 HOURS

2 tbsp sunflower oil

1 onion, finely chopped

3 cloves garlic, minced

5 cm (2 in) ginger, peeled and minced

1 red chilli (chili), deseeded and chopped

1 carrot, peeled and finely diced

275 g / 11 oz / 1 ¼ cup channa dal, soaked in water overnight then drained

500ml / 18 fl. oz / 2 cups vegetable stock

2 tsp ground cumin

2 tsp ground coriander seeds

1 tsp paprika

1 tsp turmeric

1 tsp garam masala

1 tsp amchoor (dried mango powder)

GARNISH

4 sprigs coriander (cilantro)

4 small red chillies

METHOD

- Heat the oil in a large casserole dish set over a medium heat.

- Sweat together the onion, garlic, ginger and chilli with a little salt for 6–7 minutes, stirring occasionally until softened.

- Add the ground spices and stir well, then add the lentils and the stock.

- Stir well then pour into a slow cooker and cook on a low setting for 5 hours until the lentils have absorbed the stock and the mixture is akin to a thick soup.

- Adjust the seasoning to taste then ladle into soup bowls

- Garnish with the coriander and a small chilli in each bowl.

PISTOU SOUP WITH AGED MIMOLETTE

SERVES
4

PREPARATION TIME: 15 MINUTES
COOKING TIME: 4 HOURS

2 tbsp olive oil

1 courgette, finely diced

1 clove garlic, minced

110 g / 4 oz / 1 ½ cups green beans

110 g / 4 oz / 1 cup large macaroni

225 g / 9 oz / ½ cup canned cannellini
beans, drained

110 g / 4 oz / ¼ cup canned kidney
beans, drained

30 g / 1 oz / 2 tbsp preserved peppers,
drained and chopped

500 ml / 18 fl. oz / 2 cups vegetable stock

FOR THE PISTOU

110 ml / 4 fl. oz / ½ cup olive oil

4 tbsp Parmesan, finely grated

2 tbsp basil leaves

2 cloves garlic, crushed

GARNISH

2 tbsp Mimolette, shaved

METHOD

- Heat the olive oil in a large saucepan set over a medium heat.

- Sweat the courgette and garlic together with a little seasoning for 4–5 minutes, stirring frequently.

- Add the drained beans, green beans, stock, peppers and macaroni and stir well.

- Carefully pour into a slow cooker and cook on a low setting for 4 hours.

- After 4 hours, check to make sure the macaroni is cooked through.

- Adjust the seasoning to taste and keep warm on a low setting as you prepare the pistou.

- Blend the basil leaves, Parmesan, garlic, seasoning and a little of the oil until you have a smooth paste.

- Add the rest of the oil in a slow, steady stream as you keep the motor running until you have a thickened, pesto-like texture.

- Spoon into a bowl, ready to be used.

- Ladle the soup into warm serving bowls and spoon a tablespoon of the pistou into it.

- Garnish with shavings of the Mimolette before serving.

CURRIED PUMPKIN SOUP

SERVES
4

PREPARATION TIME: 15 MINUTES
COOKING TIME: 3 HOURS 25 MINUTES

4 tbsp cup olive oil

1 kg / 2 lbs 4 oz / 6 ½ cups pumpkin, peeled,
de-seeded and cut into chunks

2 small onions, finely diced

750 ml / 1 ½ pints / 3 cups vegetable stock

1 tbsp Madras curry powder

2 tsp ground cumin

1 tsp ground coriander seeds

1 tsp Cayenne pepper

salt and pepper

GARNISH

110 g / 4 oz / 1 cup cashews, roughly chopped

METHOD

- Heat the olive oil in a large saucepan over a medium heat and sweat the onions with some salt for 6–7 minutes until they start to soften.

- Add the ground spices and stir well.

- Add the pumpkin and continue to cook for 10 minutes, stirring occasionally.

- Spoon everything into a slow cooker and cover with the stock. Cook on a low setting for 3 hours.

- Pour everything back into a saucepan and remove half of the pumpkin using a slotted spoon.

- Purée the soup until smooth using a stick blender, then add the pumpkin back into the soup.

- Adjust the seasoning to taste and ladle into warm soup bowls.

- Garnish each bowl with chopped cashews and freshly ground black pepper before serving.

PUY LENTIL SOUP

SERVES
2

PREPARATION TIME: 5 MINUTES
COOKING TIME: 1 HOUR

4 tbsp olive oil

1 red onion, very finely chopped

2 cloves of garlic, crushed

1 l / 1 pint 15 fl. oz / 4 cups vegetable stock

400 g / 14 oz / 3 ¼ cups puy lentils

2 tbsp flat leaf parsley, finely chopped

2 tbsp basil, finely chopped

salt and black pepper

METHOD

- Heat the oil in a large saucepan and fry the onion for 5 minutes over a medium heat. Add the garlic and cook for 1 minute.

- Stir in the stock and lentils then simmer for 45 minutes or until the lentils are tender. If the liquid evaporates too quickly, add a little boiling water.

- Taste for seasoning and add salt and black pepper as necessary then stir in the herbs and serve.

CARROT AND APPLE SOUP

SERVES
4

PREPARATION TIME: 15 MINUTES
COOKING TIME: 3 HOURS 20–25 MINUTES

30 g / 1 oz / ¼ stick unsalted butter

30 ml / 1 fl. oz / 2 tbsp olive oil

1 kg / 2 lbs 4 oz / 6 ½ cups sweet potato, peeled and diced

2 cloves of garlic, minced

500 ml / 18 fl. oz / 2 cups vegetable stock

125 ml / 4 ½ fl. oz / ½ cup carrot juice

125 ml / 4 ½ fl. oz / ½ cup double (heavy) cream

55 ml / 2 fl. oz / ¼ cup apple juice

salt and pepper

METHOD

- Melt the butter with the olive oil in a large saucepan set over a medium heat.

- Add the garlic and sweet potato and sweat with a little salt for 15–20 minutes, stirring occasionally, until the sweet potato is soft.

- Spoon everything into a slow cooker and cover with the stock, carrot and apple juice.

- Cook on a low setting for 3 hours.

- After 3 hours, pour everything back into a saucepan and purée using a stick blender until smooth.

- Add the double cream, stir well until incorporated then warm over a low heat for 5 minutes.

- Ladle into soup bowls and serve immediately.

CREAM OF PUMPKIN AND TOMATO SOUP

SERVES
4

PREPARATION TIME: 15 MINUTES
COOKING TIME: 3 HOURS 20 MINUTES

4 tbsp olive oil

1 kg / 2 lb 4 oz / 6 ½ cups pumpkin, peeled,
de-seeded and cut into chunks

2 onions, finely diced

500 ml / 18 fl. oz / 2 cups vegetable stock

200 ml / 7 fl. oz / ⅘ cup double (heavy) cream

1 tsp ground pink peppercorns

4 fresh tomatoes, chopped

GARNISH

1 tbsp pink peppercorns, lightly crushed

METHOD

- Heat the olive oil in a large saucepan over a medium heat and sweat the onions with some salt and the ground pink peppercorns for 6–7 minutes until they start to soften.

- Add the pumpkin and tomatoes and continue to cook for 10 minutes, stirring occasionally.

- Spoon everything into a slow cooker and cover with the stock.

- Cook on a low setting for 3 hours.

- Pour everything back into a saucepan, stir through the cream and simmer the mixture for 5 minutes.

- Purée the soup with a stick blender until smooth.

- Adjust the seasoning and then ladle into serving bowls.

- Garnish each bowl with a pinch of the crushed peppercorns before serving.

CHUNKY VEGETABLE SOUP

SERVES
2

PREPARATION TIME: 5 MINUTES
COOKING TIME: 20 MINUTES

2 tbsp olive oil

2 leeks, sliced

2 cloves of garlic, crushed

4 spring onions, chopped

2 courgettes (zucchini), chopped

1 red pepper, sliced

1 orange pepper, chopped

150 g / 5 ½ oz / 1 cup broad beans,
defrosted if frozen

1 litre / 1 pint 15 fl. oz / 4 cups vegetable stock

a few sprigs of flat leaf parsley to serve

METHOD

• Heat the oil in a saucepan and fry the leeks for 5 minutes or until softened.

• Add the garlic and vegetables to the pan and cook for 2 more minutes, then stir in the vegetable stock and bring to the boil.

• Simmer for 10 minutes then season to taste with salt and pepper.

• Ladle the soup into 4 warm bowls and garnish with parsley.

SPLIT PEA SOUP

SERVES
4

PREPARATION TIME: 5 MINUTES
COOKING TIME: 1 HOUR

2 tbsp olive oil

2 tbsp butter

1 onion, finely chopped

2 cloves of garlic, crushed

100 g / 3 ½ oz / ½ cup dried green split peas

1 litre / 1 pint 15 fl. oz / 4 cups vegetable stock

300 g / 10 ½ oz / 2 cups garden peas,
defrosted if frozen

100 ml / 3 ½ fl. oz / ½ cup double
(heavy) cream

parsley leaves, to garnish

salt and freshly ground black pepper

METHOD

• Heat the oil and butter in a saucepan and fry the onion for 5 minutes or until softened.

• Add the garlic and split peas to the pan and cook for 2 more minutes, then stir in the vegetable stock.

• Simmer for 45 minutes or until the split peas are starting to break down, then add the garden peas. Simmer for 5 minutes or until tender, then remove a few of the peas to use as a garnish.

• Blend the soup until smooth with a liquidiser or immersion blender then taste and adjust the seasoning with salt and pepper.

• Ladle into warm bowls and add a swirl of cream to each one. Garnish with the reserved peas and a few parsley leaves.

FENNEL SOUP

SERVES
4

PREPARATION TIME: 15 MINUTES
COOKING TIME: 4 HOURS

3 tbsp olive oil

4 fennel bulbs, finely sliced

2 sticks celery, finely sliced

1 leek, finely sliced and washed

2 medium white potatoes, peeled and diced

500 ml / 18 fl. oz / 2 cups
vegetable stock

GARNISH

2 chive stalks, finely chopped

METHOD

- Heat the olive oil in a large casserole dish set over a medium heat.

- Sweat the fennel, celery and leek with a little seasoning for 10–12 minutes, stirring frequently, until softened.

- Add the potato and stock and stir well.

- Pour everything into a slow cooker and cook on a low setting for 4 hours.

- After 4 hours remove a little of the leek which will act as a garnish.

- Purée with a stick blender until smooth.

- Adjust the seasoning to taste then ladle into warm soup bowls.

- Garnish with the leek and chives before serving.

CREAM OF TOMATO SOUP

SERVES
4

PREPARATION TIME: 20 MINUTES
COOKING TIME: 3 HOURS 30 MINUTES

2 tbsp olive oil

1 kg / 2 lb 4 oz / 4 cups tomatoes, cored and quartered

1 onion, finely chopped

2 tbsp tomato purée

1 bay leaf

1 tsp dried basil

1.2 l / 2 pints / 4 4/5 cups vegetable stock, hot

125 ml / 4 ½ fl. oz / ½ cup double (heavy) cream

GARNISH

2 tbsp double (heavy) cream

4 sprigs basil leaves

METHOD

- Heat the olive oil in a large saucepan over a medium-low heat for 1–2 minutes.

- Add the onion and sweat for 8–10 minutes with a little salt. Stir in the tomato purée, then add the tomatoes.

- Add the bay leaf, dried basil and seasoning and cover the pot, allowing the tomatoes to stew for 10 minutes.

- Remove the cover after ten minutes and stir in the stock. Pour everything into a slow cooker and cook on a low setting for 3 hours.

- Pour everything from the slow cooker into a large saucepan. Discard the bay leaf.

- Blend the soup using a stick blender until smooth, then stir through the cream. Adjust the seasoning to taste.

- Ladle into bowls and garnish with a swirl of cream and a sprig of basil. Serve immediately.

MUSHROOM SOUP

SERVES
4

PREPARATION TIME: 15 MINUTES
COOKING TIME: 4 HOURS

600g mixed wild mushrooms, chopped

30 ml / 2 tbsp vegetable oil

salt and pepper

2 clove garlic, minced

1 large onion, finely chopped

110g / 4 oz / ½ cup leeks, finely chopped

500ml / 16 fl. oz / 2 cups veg stock

1 tbsp turmeric

2 medium potatoes, finely chopped

1 bay leaf

100ml / 3 fl. oz / ½ cup single cream

salt and ground black pepper

1 tbsp fine chopped mushrooms fried

METHOD

• Heat the oil in a pan. Fry the onion, garlic, leeks, turmeric and mushrooms for 8 minutes stirring gently.

• Transfer to the crockpot and add all the other ingredients.

• Cover and cook on medium for 4 hours.

• Taste and adjust seasoning.

• Serve in individual bowls and garnished with 1 tbsp chopped fried mushrooms.

VEGGIE BOUILLABAISSE

SERVES
4

PREPARATION TIME: 10–15 MINUTES
COOKING TIME: 4 HOURS 20 MINUTES

55 ml / 2 fl. oz / ¼ cup olive oil

4 fennel bulbs, trimmed and chopped

1 leek, sliced and washed

4 carrots, peeled and sliced

2 large white potatoes, peeled and diced

500 ml / 18 fl. oz / 2 cups vegetable stock

400 g / 14 oz / 2 cups canned chopped tomatoes

salt and pepper

GARNISH

sprigs of basil leaves

1 tbsp picked thyme leaves

METHOD

- Heat the olive oil in a large saucepan set over a medium heat until hot.

- Sweat the fennel, leek, potato and carrots for 8–10 minutes, stirring occasionally until softened.

- Add the stock and chopped tomatoes with some seasoning.

- Stir well before pouring into a slow cooker.

- Cover with a lid and cook on a medium setting for 4 hours until the vegetables are soft.

- Adjust the seasoning to taste before ladling into serving bowls and garnishing with a sprinkling of thyme leaves and a sprig of basil.

FISH

SEAFOOD SOUP

SERVES
4

PREPARATION TIME: 20 MINUTES
COOKING TIME: 3 HOURS 15 MINUTES

2 tbsp olive oil

2 cloves garlic, minced

2 bulbs fennel, trimmed and finely chopped

300g / 10 ½ oz / 2 cups prawns (shrimps),
peeled and deveined

2 sea bass fillets, pin-boned and
cut into chunks

150 g / 5 oz / 1 cup squid rings

150 g / 5 oz / 1 ½ cups cooked
mussel meat

500 ml / 18 fl. oz / 2 cups fish stock

250 ml / 9 fl. oz / 1 cup passata

125 ml / 4 ½ fl. oz / ½ cup white wine

1 bay leaf

4 sprigs tarragon

GARNISH

1 tbsp tarragon leaves, finely chopped

1 tbsp chervil leaves, finely chopped

METHOD

- Heat the olive oil in a large saucepan set over a moderate heat until hot and sweat the garlic and fennel for 4–5 minutes, stirring occasionally until softened.

- Spoon into a slow cooker and all the remaining ingredients apart from the chopped herbs and mussel meat.

- Cook on a low setting for 3 hours until the fish and seafood is tender and cooked; the soup should be thickened. If not, remove some of the liquid using a ladle.

- Adjust the seasoning to taste and discard the bay leaf.

- Add the mussel meat and warm through for 10 minutes.

- Spoon into serving bowls and garnish with the chopped herbs before serving.

CURRIED PRAWN SOUP IN COCONUT SHELL

SERVES
4

PREPARATION TIME: 20 MINUTES
COOKING TIME: 4 HOURS

2 tbsp sunflower oil

2 shallots, finely chopped

4 cloves garlic, chopped

10cm (4 in) piece of lemongrass, chopped

5cm (2 in) ginger, peeled and chopped

2 green chillies, deseeded and chopped

500 ml / 18 fl. oz / 2 cups coconut milk

250 ml / 9 fl. oz / 1 cup fish stock

8 king prawns

300 g / 10 ½ oz / 2 cups dried shrimp, thawed

1 tbsp Madras curry powder

1 tsp ground cinnamon

1 tsp turmeric

½ tsp paprika

1 tbsp light brown sugar

1 lime, juiced

1 tbsp fish sauce

GARNISH

4 sprigs of Thai basil leaves

METHOD

- Combine the shallot, garlic, lemongrass, ginger, chilli, sunflower oil and seasoning in a food processor.

- Pulse until smooth then add the ground spices and sugar and pulse again until you have a paste.

- Heat the paste in a large saucepan set over a medium heat, stirring frequently for 2–3 minutes.

- Add the coconut milk and fish stock and whisk well until you have a broth.

- Pour into a slow cooker and add the shrimp and prawns.

- Cook on a low setting for 4 hours.

- Adjust the seasoning after 4 hours using lime juice, fish sauce, salt and pepper.

- Serve in hollowed out coconut halves (if available).

- Garnish with the basil leaves before serving.

CLAM CHOWDER

SERVES
4

PREPARATION TIME: 10 MINUTES
COOKING TIME: 4 HOURS

450 g / 1 lb / 3 cups clams, cleaned

1 cooked lobster tail, cut into chunks

75 ml / 3 fl. oz / ⅓ cup water

55 g / 2 oz / ½ stick unsalted butter

110 g / 4 oz / ¼ cup thickly sliced
bacon, chopped

4 small onions, sliced

3 large white potatoes, peeled and finely diced

250 ml / 9 fl. oz / 1 cup whole milk

125 ml / 4 ½ fl. oz / ½ cup double
(heavy) cream

500 ml / 18 fl. oz / 2 cups fish stock

1 bay leaf

pinch ground nutmeg

METHOD

- Place a saucepan over a high heat and add the clams and water.

- Cover with a lid and cook for 2–3 minutes until the clams have opened; discard any that don't open.

- Strain the clams in a colander and collect the cooking liquor in a bowl underneath.

- Remove the clams from their shells and reserve to one side.

- Melt the butter in a large saucepan set over a medium heat and sauté the bacon until it browns, stirring occasionally.

- Add the onions and cook for a further 2–3 minutes until they start to soften.

- Add the potatoes, milk, cream, bay leaf, cooking juice and stock from the clams and nutmeg.

- Pour into a slow cooker and cook on a low setting for 4 hours until the potato starts to break down.

- Fish out the bay leaf and discard.

- Purée the mixture very briefly with a stick blender until you have thick soup-like texture.

- Stir the clams and lobster into the chowder and adjust the seasoning to taste.

- Spoon into serving bowls and serve immediately.

CURRY AND SHRIMP SOUP

SERVES
4

PREPARATION TIME: 15 MINUTES
COOKING TIME: 4 HOURS

2 tbsp groundnut oil

300 g / 10 ½ oz / 2 cups prawns (shrimps)

150 g / 5 oz / 2 ½ oz baby spinach

500 ml / 18 fl. oz / 2 cups fish stock

1 turnip, peeled and diced

1 tsp Madras curry powder

1 tsp paprika

½ tsp Cayenne pepper

2 sticks of celery, sliced

2 tbsp pumpkin seeds, lightly toasted

1 tbsp soy sauce

1 tbsp fish sauce

METHOD

• Heat the groundnut oil in a large saucepan set over a medium heat until hot.

• Sweat the celery and turnip for 6–7 minutes, stirring occasionally, until they start to soften.

• Add the ground spices and stir well.

• Add all the remaining ingredients apart from the baby spinach, then pour carefully into a slow cooker.

• Cook on a low setting for 4 hours.

• After 4 hours, add the spinach and stir well.

• Let it wilt, then turn off the slow cooker once wilted.

• Adjust the seasoning to taste before ladling into warm soup bowls.

• Serve immediately.

VEGETABLE AND COD MINESTRONE SOUP

SERVES
2

PREPARATION TIME: 20 MINUTES
COOKING TIME: 1 HOUR

1 tbsp olive oil

70 g / 2 ¾ oz / ½ cup pancetta or smoked
streaky bacon, chopped

1 onion, peeled and finely chopped

1 carrot, peeled and finely chopped

2 celery stalks, finely chopped

2 potatoes, peeled and finely chopped

2 tomatoes, finely chopped

1 L / 2 ½ pints / 5 cups chicken stock

60 g / 1 ½ oz / ¼ cup macaroni pasta

40 g / 1 oz frozen peas

1 courgette (zucchini), finely chopped

400g / 13 ½ oz / 1 ½ cups cod loin

salt and pepper

extra virgin olive oil

METHOD

- Heat the olive oil in a pan and cook the pancetta until the fat runs and it starts to turn golden.

- Add the onion, carrot and celery and cook until softened and translucent.

- Continue to add the potatoes and tomatoes and cook for a few minutes.

- Add the stock and simmer for 30 minutes until all the vegetables are tender.

- Once simmered, add the pasta and cook for a further 20 minutes.

- Finish with adding the peas, courgette and gently lower the fish into the soup and cook for another 10 minutes.

- Ladle into bowls to serve, drizzled with oil.

SEAFOOD MINESTRONE

SERVES
4

PREPARATION TIME: 10 MINUTES
COOKING TIME: 35–40 MINUTES

1 tbsp olive oil

1 onion, peeled and finely chopped

1 carrot, peeled and finely chopped

1 celery stalk, peeled and chopped

2 tomatoes, finely chopped

1 L / 2 pints / 4 ¼ cups chicken stock

50 g / 1 ½ oz / ¼ cup macaroni pasta

750 g / 1 ¼ lb / 3 cups mixed raw seafood, such as prawns, scallops, mussels and squid

1 bunch parsley, chopped

½ lemon

salt and pepper

METHOD

• Heat the olive oil in a pan and sweat the onion, carrot and celery without colouring for 5 minutes.

• Add the tomatoes and cook for a further 2 minutes.

• Pour over the stock, bring to a simmer and add the pasta.

• Cook for about 20 minutes until the pasta is tender.

• Add the seafood and poach in the soup until the prawns turn pink, the scallops opaque and the mussels open. Discard any that remain closed.

• Scatter over the parsley and adjust the seasoning.

SARDINE BOUILLABAISSE

SERVES
4

PREPARATION TIME: 15–20 MINUTES
COOKING TIME: 6 HOURS 15 MINUTES

55 ml / 2 fl. oz / ¼ cup olive oil

450 g / 1 lb sardines in brine, drained

500 ml / 18 fl. oz / 2 cups fish stock

400 g / 14 oz / 2 cups canned chopped tomatoes

1 tbsp tomato purée

1 large white potato, peeled and sliced thinly

1 fennel bulb, trimmed and sliced

2 onion finely chopped

4 cloves garlic, minced

sprigs of thyme, to garnish

1 bay leaf

salt and black pepper

METHOD

- Heat the olive oil in a large casserole dish over a moderate heat.

- Sweat the onion, garlic for 10 minutes with a little salt, stirring occasionally until they are soft but not coloured. Stir in the tomato purée, fennel seeds, canned chopped tomatoes and bay leaf. Stir well and cover with the fish stock and 1 cup of water.

- Pour into a slow cooker and cover with a lid. Cook on a medium setting for 2 hours.

- Strain into a large, clean saucepan, pressing the tomatoes and all other ingredients through the sieve to extract as much flavour as possible. Add the potato and sliced fennel and pour back into the slow cooker. Add the sardines and cover with a lid.

- Cook on a medium setting for a further 4 hours until the fish is cooked. Adjust the seasoning as necessary, then ladle into a serving dish.

- Garnish with sprigs of thyme before serving.

HADDOCK SOUP

SERVES
4

PREPARATION TIME: 15–20 MINUTES
COOKING TIME: 4 HOURS 25–30 MINUTES

4 x 175 g / 6 oz skinless haddock fillets

150 g / 5 oz / 1 cup mussels, cleaned

30 ml / 1 fl. oz / 2 tbsp olive oil

1 onion, chopped

2 cloves garlic, minced

1 bay leaf

300 g / 10 ½ oz / 2 cups new potatoes

500 ml / 18 fl. oz / 2 cups vegetable stock

400 g / 14 oz / 2 cups canned chopped tomatoes

sprigs of thyme, to garnish

salt and pepper

METHOD

- Parboil the potatoes in a large saucepan of boiling, salted water for 10 minutes.
  Drain and allow to cool.

- Heat the olive oil in a large casserole dish over a medium heat. Sauté the onion and garlic
  for 4–5 minutes, stirring occasionally, until softened.

- Add the chopped tomatoes, bay leaf and vegetables stock and stir well. Cut the potatoes
  in half, then add to the stew.

- Pour into a slow cooker and add the mussels and haddock. Cook on a medium setting
  for 4 hours. Remove the lid and discard any mussels that haven't opened. Discard the bay
  leaf, then adjust the seasoning.

- Spoon into serving bowls and remove the leaves from some of the thyme sprigs.
  Sprinkle on top, then garnish with sprigs of thyme before serving.

COD AND CHICKPEA SOUP

SERVES
4

PREPARATION TIME: 25 MINUTES
COOKING TIME: 6 HOURS

600 g / 1 lb 5 oz salt cod tripe

plain (all-purpose) flour for dusting

1 onion finely chopped

1 x 400 g can cooked chickpeas (garbanzo beans)

120 ml / 4 fl. oz / ½ cup white wine

4 cloves of garlic, minced

15 ml / 1 tbsp sunflower oil

15 ml / 0.5 fl. oz / 1 tbsp butter

1 pinch saffron soaked in 120 ml / 4 fl. oz / 0.5 cup fish stock

100 g / 4 oz peas

salt and pepper

METHOD

- Drain the salt cod or tripe from the soaking water and pat dry with kitchen towel and dust with flour.

- Heat the oil in a pan and sauté the cod pieces, dusted in flour for 3 minutes each side until golden – remove with a slotted spoon into the slow cooker.

- Gently sauté the onion and garlic until golden brown.

- Add the white wine and boil deglaze pan and burn off alcohol. Add fish stock coloured with saffron and peas and bring gently to the boil.

- Pour into the slow cooker and cook on a low setting for 6 hours.

- Pour in the chickpeas and allow to warm through thoroughly. Adjust the seasoning to taste.

- Spoon into serving dishes and garnish with the parsley and freshly ground black pepper. Serve immediately with crusty bread or vegetables.